MIGHT FORGET AFTER READING

NURAIN F K

Made with ♥ on the Notion Press Platform
www.notionpress.com

Throughout my life, I've witnessed people dedicating precious things to those they love, those who have supported them during difficult times, or their life journey. I had decided to follow a similar path, but then it occurred to me: 'Why not dedicate this book to myself?' I believe this book should be a gift to oneself.

We often fail to acknowledge or praise our accomplishments and endeavours. Some of the poems contain stanzas dedicated to specific individuals. However, I dedicate this book to myself for simply being who I am and for never giving up. So I urge all readers to consider this book a gift to themselves. This book stands as a significant achievement not only for my present self but also for the young poet who embarked on this journey at the age of eleven.

Contents

Contents

Contents

Preface

Dear________________,

Hey, looks like you found my book! Well, I know poetry has been made super serious for ages now, but don't worry, you don't need to dissect and annotate my poems unless you want to.

This book is not going to help you understand the meaning of life, nor give you the experience of a 'Eureka' moment. It might just simply remind you of the relatable experiences that you have in your day-to-day life, and tell you that everyone goes through the same thing at some point of time in their lives too.

We all are built in a way that makes us want to be included in the social circle, but alone and guarded too. That is why I don't want you to look at this book as a literary piece of work or a guide to life, but, the unsaid feelings of a little girl who is now growing up to the responsibilities of life and adulting.

Hope you enjoy the journey ahead and feel a little at ease about the entire 'growing up' and 'surviving' journey.
Take care <3

Lots of love XOXO,
Nurain

Acknowledgements

Although I dedicate this book to myself, there are a few people who made it possible for this book to be complete. Whether it was helping me proofread, or maybe even designing the cover, these few people are the reason why 'Might forget after reading', is in your hands right now.

Deep thanks to the following:

- My mother Nadia Khakiyani, always helped me correct my mistakes and stood by me on this journey.
- Adya Red, my friend and illustrator, combined my imagination and her talent to add life to the book cover.
- An Angel who wished to stay anonymous, but played the biggest part in taking out time to completely proofread and carefully suggest changes, to enhance the readability of the poems.
- Dr. Meera Baindur, my college professor, proofread my work and corrected me as and when necessary.
- B Dhanushree and Arushi, my schoolmates, with whom I wrote the poem, 'Roar of his soul'.
- Skanda my friend and fellow poet, whose opinions and suggestions changed my way of thinking and writing.
- My family members and close friends, who have always motivated me and pushed me to publish this book. I wish I could mention each name here specifically, but then the acknowledgements page would be longer than the book itself.
- And last but not least, all those people who have read and liked my poems either online or in person, for making me feel that sharing my poems with the world matters.

The Beginning

This part includes the journey of my 11-year-old self.

1. Childhood

Do you remember having one?
A childhood filled with fun.
ABC and 123,
And sitting on the mango tree.

Running, playing all day long,
Life was like a merry song.
Butterflies everywhere,
They were so pretty to stare.

Games, toys, things to play,
Without these, there wasn't a day.
No tension and no stress,
Only play and make a mess.

Pretty dresses and pretty bows,
And trying to bend and touch your toes.
Everyone knew how to share and care,
It was just me and my teddy bear.

Life has come a long way,
All these flashbacks make my day,
And I now pray,
For those lovely memories to stay.

~*~

2. Goal

What is a goal?
It is life's major role.
It gives you a part to play,
And prevents you from going astray.

It makes you strong,
And shows that no one can prove you wrong.
The knowledge makes you powerful,
And the results are delightful.

A goal is like a sense of direction,
A way to correct the imperfection.
So if you have done your part,
There is now another journey to start.

~*~

3. Magic

We all have magic in us,
It has to be found.
It is in and out,
It is all around.

It is in what you do,
It is in what you see.
It is in the future,
It is in our memory.

It is there in joy,
It is in pain,
It is in winter,
It is in rain.

We can feel it,
We can experience it.
We can embrace it.
And also conceal it.

It is all powerful,
It is graceful.
It is magically,
Extremely wonderful.

It is generally pure,
And sometimes harmful.
But, it itself is the cure,
And saves you from what's awful.

We realize its presence,
When we sacrifice our desire.
And understand its essence,
As the bar keeps getting higher.

We all have magic in us,
We just need to try and discover.
There is no need to rush,
Because one day the wait will be over.

~*~

4. Teacher

More than a leader,
A teacher is a preacher.
They are always there to guide,
And their students are their pride.

They are with you come what may,
Even though they don't always stay.
Their teachings won't let us go astray.
And the knowledge imparted will stay till D-day.

They love us immense,
And also make us work intense.
They do care,
And when we need them they are there.

They don't just have brains but beauty,
And have taught us to fulfill our duty.
They have made our minds pretty,
And filled our lives with simplicity.

They have been there as a parent,
When our parents weren't physically present.
They are a fire,
That everyone admire!

~*~

5. Start over

When is the right time?
To know that things are over.
When memories are as sour as lime,
And people feel bitter.

Sweet thoughts disappear,
When you're grave and have fear.
When you can't see things clear,
And all the problems you have are not so dear.

When things go wrong,
When there are days that don't get along.
When you don't feel strong,
And the journey is long.

Love is far away,
Troubles are here to stay.
When it's all about pause or play,
And the penalty you have to pay.

We should begin from the start,
And tear our fears apart.
I know things are hard,
And life's like a tarot card.

It is hard to start over,
And forget the past.
And search for a four-leafed clover,
Because this world is vast.

~*~

6. Choices

At this point of time in the night,
I think my decision was right.
That I have to fight,
To prove that I am bright.

As I sit here alone,
Something of mine has been torn.
Not just my heart but my soul,
And all my choices have been made troll.

I could scream and shout,
But how will that help me out?
I could cry and feel remorse,
But that would just make things worse.

I have no idea what to choose,
Because whatever I have, I'd lose.
All my dreams and my fate,
Will either shut or open that gate.

My life is stuck here,
And it's all because of my fear.
As the path ahead isn't clear,
And the choice I have to make is coming near.

I can't stop to think,
Or even to blink,
I have to go on,
From dusk to dawn.

I will rise above them all,
And always stand tall.
As the choice that I install,
Will not let me fall.

~*~

7. Friends

Why do we have friends?
Are they only for trends?
Or are they people who help us mend,
Our life stories till the end?

We meet many people everywhere,
And have some emotions to share.
There are a few who care,
And some who just sit and stare.

Some people are flatterers, some are foe,
And some who easily go.
Some we meet and some we see,
Each one has their own misery.

We see strangers every day,
All of them have stories to share,
And when we reach the story's end,
We tend to find a special friend.

~*~

8. Fear

Everyone has fears,
Those fears fill their cheeks with tears.
I have a fear,
But I won't get scared as I know God is here.

With fear comes tension,
And some are too scary to mention.
Your life seems depress,
And this gives rise to a lot of stress.

It is caused in many ways,
And as you grow, it fades but yet it stays.
Fear gets sorrow,
That you start to question whether you will survive tomorrow?

Your life starts seeming slow,
But the fear, it would only grow.
You may get trapped,
And to you, it gets strapped.

When it comes, you feel like crying,
That you have the idea, of dying.
When your loved one is close,
Fear gives you a little less dose.

When someone is there,
Your fear is aware.
You go mad,
And looking at you people feel sad.

Never let it touch
Your heart, very much.
When it strikes just pray,
That may this fear go away.

~*~

Growth

Let us continue the journey with my teenage self....

9. Hear Me

"Hey, how are you? What are you doing?"
"How's your day going? Are you stressed?"
"Are you free? I wanted to talk…"
Sorry not now, but will let you know when I am.

I waited and waited and waited.
Not a message was received nor a call heard.
I'd shout on a stormy night,
To you, I seemed chirpy and bright,
But only I know how my fists were clenched,
And my chest felt tight.

My expressions were talking, did you hear?
My mouth was twitching, did you see?
To you, I was always crazy happy,
But I know that my heart was screaming.

You saw my smile and felt its warmth,
My mouth went dry but I was shouting.
Call you later, will talk soon.
Was I the only one to start the conversation and call?
Did you care when I went mute?
Or were you happy that now there's no one to bother you?

We used to be so close and talk every single day,
Now you found someone better and left me hanging there.
I ain't complaining or blaming you,
I am just asking whether anything that you ever said was true.

~*~

10. I'm so over you

The last words I heard before zoning out,
Last words I never thought would flow out of your mouth.
I always cared and you called me 'clingy',
That's the price I got for my love, well then you are 'stingy'.

Star gazing became one of my distractions,
And I started to analyze all your past words and actions.
All those doubts and suspicions started to make sense,
And you and your secrets were highly dense.

My love for you made me a complete mess,
But yours compared to mine was day by day less.
Was it someone else? Or was I hard to bear?
You always said that 'I was unique, precious, and rare'.

Am I sad or do I regret?
But now I know that YOU will be easy to forget.
"I'm so over you", that's what you said,
You're now a forgotten memory, a mistake I should never repeat ahead.

~*~

11. You know

I hate those people you know,
Those that temporarily walk into your life, suddenly turn around and go.
No reason whatsoever,
But completely change your life forever.

You don't get the chance to ask any question,
And you start to hate every vibe or sensation.
Start, stop, pause, and play,
This is how your life feels like every day.

No restart, no other chance,
Just pick a side while the others glance.
You forget what you have to say,
As this time you want the person to stay.

Life's a game, now that's true,
And you don't have time to think it through.
'Please comeback', is now forgotten,
And your expressions and thoughts are now rotten.

Happiness and companionship, what's that?
When you've lost conscience to choose between this or that.
For now, let's pause,
As we have to identify our purpose and cause.

Though we can't start over,
Let's create a new chapter.
Let's fall to learn, and not to break,
Let's learn to move on, this time not just for sake.

~*~

12. Inevitable attachment

I asked him about her,
He replied 'She is still so dear'.
Her touch and her hold,
Made him feel confident and bold.

He said 'It were her eyes',
That remarkably hypnotize.
Her stare made him melt,
And every problem was dealt.

He said she deserves the best,
And when she's around, he forgets the rest.
She is composed and warm,
And her presence keeps him away from the storm.

She's his safe place,
And he rests assured in her embrace.
He trusts her more than the world,
And holding his finger she twirled.

He narrated his experience to me,
And smiled at the thought of this inevitable memory.
He was my grandfather,
And she was his ultimate forever, his significant other.

~*~

13. Mysterious Guy

A night of clinking of glasses,
And loud blasting music.
And giving you constant glances,
While the next morning I woke up sick.

You caught my attention,
And knocked me off my feet.
The mysterious guy, I now mention
To my friends, whenever I speak.

Those shiny eyes,
That looked back at me once in a while.
Amongst all the other guys,
I noticed his perfect smile.

He was with a girl,
But he kept glancing at me.
They danced and she'd twirl,
Till I no longer could see.

The night went by,
As I kept gulping down.
She waved you goodbye,
And your eyes returned on me now.

I was about to leave,
And felt a sudden grip.
That familiar rolled-up sleeve,
Made my heart skip.

Those eyes again,
Woke me up from my partial slumber.
As you walked me to my lane,
Took my hand, and stuffed your number.

~*~

14. The Scale

Chubby, fat, and cellulite,
Is that what affects your thoughts and sight?
Do you see crooked teeth,
Or complain about dry and chapped feet?

More than needed body hair,
And if they need to be whitewashed to look fair.
Keeping pretty polished nails,
Or weighing your worth on different scales.

Strict dietary plans and restrictions,
And for glowing skin, water infused with lemons,
Paying thousands to have not a single pimple,
But skin naturally has cuts, spots and wrinkles.

Do you see oily hair or hair fall?
But the clothes that are repeated, you recall.
The fashion sense you criticise,
And whether or not clothes fit their size.

Botox and different plastic surgeries to try,
In the end, to our bodies, we lie.
How many standards more?
To reach the perfect beauty score.

We all have different shapes and size,
So why distinguish and criticise?
You won't match mine and I won't yours,
So let's accept each other with open arms.

~*~

15. Roar of his soul

Oh dear oh dear!
Why do we forget that even men have fear?
Why are they expected to excel in all spheres?
And why does the society ignore all their tears?

He's macho, he's the man,
And it's said that every lady is his fan.
Handsome, smart, and rich, is that all we perceive?
Are these titles all that he deserves to achieve?

How much does he earn?
Is that your only concern?
Is he strong or is he weak?
If he doesn't speak much doesn't mean he's a geek.

Not just offended but he too feels hurt,
And sometimes even his tensions need to blurt.
For the society, like a lion, he is raised,
But if he doesn't roar, he isn't praised.

They too have ups and downs, highs and lows,
And have to create a stance in the society as time goes.
They can have stress, anxiety, pressure, and depression,
But have been taught to suppress their expression.

We have to support each other hand in hand,
So that people can broaden their minds to understand.
We are involved in the part and parcel of life and so are they,
That's why let's take these ideals and hypocrisy, and throw them away.

~*~

16. I'm not her

I'm not her,
But you told me to try.
She is perfect,
Is that why?

Drinking only water,
And forcing myself to starve.
Is beauty defined in only,
Figures and curves?

I was looking at you,
But you were admiring her.
Her one smile,
Was enough for your heart to flutter.

You flashed her a smile,
The one I had never seen.
But you were cold to me,
The way you had always been.

You had fallen for her,
And everyone besides me knew.
As you would lie to me,
And prove their assumptions, as untrue.

Even if I were the only one left,
You wouldn't have chosen me,
Because I am not her,
And you know I'll never be.

~*~

17. Clutched a blade

She desired warmth,
For her heart and mind.
But things went south,
And she was always left behind.

The moment she felt a little attached,
The person didn't stay.
Her relation with trust detached,
And gloom overpowered every day.

A flamed up lighter,
Not a cigar close by.
She wanted to think brighter,
But didn't want to keep her hopes high.

Her sadness turned into a poem,
Heartbreak turned into rage.
She wanted to get over them,
And lock her heart in a cage.

Rage was growing,
As love was about to fade.
Her heart, she tried sewing,
But the next day her hands clutched a blade.

Blood all around,
Messed up feeling.
But tranquility wasn't found,
As she tried to stop healing.

~*~

18. Sunflowers bloom in July

They say the dead get more flowers,
While the alive stay ignored.
You'd keep thinking for hours,
About the people you once adored.

If holding on was that difficult,
And giving up was that easy,
We'd blame it on being an adult,
And everybody would feel queasy.

Fell out of love,
That's what it's called.
Did you just shove,
All the memories due to which "we" evolved?

Moved on,
Found someone better.
Leaving me to drown,
And letting my heart shatter.

Please stay,
Give me another chance.
You said, "Go away,
I need to advance".

Now that I'm gone,
You'd see my picture and cry.
Sitting there so alone,
You'd remember us see the sunflowers bloom in July.

~*~

19. Tranquil

It was silent,
Not a word spoken.
Her thoughts were violent,
But she was broken.

She wanted a safe place,
Someone to lean on.
Someone to embrace,
But she had none.

A hand to hold,
A path to guide.
But she was told,
Feelings, what are they? Never mind.

Her words were heard,
Only by her reflection.
She was a songbird,
Now filled with emptiness and dejection.

Faded memories,
A lost voice.
Her long gone melodies,
Nothing left to rejoice.

Now silence seemed comforting,
People around felt distant.
She was growing,
Without any assistance.

~*~

20. Did I ?

Every time I look in the mirror,
I ask myself this question.
Am I just a pushover?
Or was I ever worth any attention?

Growing up has always been hard,
Everyone around knew that too.
Should I let down my guard,
To be a part of them too?

Every day I tried to be my best self,
Fought the monsters in and out.
Just so that I could add a trophy to that shelf,
But did anyone care when I was stuck in this drought?

Laughing to hide the scar,
Working hard to spread my name.
Why does everything I want seem so far?
Is this all worth it to achieve that fame?

Made promises that would lessen my pain,
Tried to soar up so high.
Did I gain?
Or was this a warning, that I knew I could only try?

I bore my feelings inside,
And held my head up high.
Just to leave the wounds behind,
Did I reach there? Did I?

~*~

21. Breakaway

The morning sunshine,
The cold dew.
The hope that everything will be fine,
Not a problem new.

The joggers on,
The sweats zipped up.
All the drowsiness gone,
And legs that won't stop.

A mini backpack,
Some essentials too.
To follow a new track,
Away from the grey and blue.

The journey was long,
As the sun spread the burning heat.
This time nothing would go wrong,
Because now I will follow my heartbeat.

The world slowly awake,
The noise coming alive.
We all were taking a break,
To kick start and strive.

The breakaway,
The coming through.
This time I won't stay,
As there are several dreams that I need to pursue.

~*~

22. Warmth

Hands cupping the hot coffee mug,
Oh that longing for a warm hug!
Rubbing the palms to create heat,
Just how would it feel, when you and I meet?

Sniffing the vanilla scent in the air,
How would it feel when you gently stroke my hair?
Wearing socks to give warmth to my feet,
Just thinking about you increases my heartbeat.

The hot cocoa, and s'mores too,
Leads my mind to again think about you.
The jacket around to protect me from the cold,
Oh, just how would it feel to be wrapped up in your hold?

The constant scrolls,
The cuddled blanket rolls,
The Pinterest saves,
And listening to heat waves.

Just how cold is the other side of the bed!
Would you accept me and let me lay my head?
Our intertwined fingers are better than heat gloves,
And cuddling while reading the story about the turtledoves.

The coffee mug now empty, the candles all melt,
Just trying to reminisce, about the way you smelt.
Need someone to hold me before the storm,
So will you be the one, and make me feel warm?

~*~

23. Just a phase

Studies, studies every day,
No time to just sit or lay.
Back pain and neck pain,
This is getting insane!

You say ten chapters,
I'm stuck on a page.
Each mark matters,
I'm too young to die at this age!

Plans just canceled and birthdays missed,
Please just one break, I insist!
Coffee became my new buddy,
To sit all night while trying to study.

Netflix and chill?
While my marks go downhill.
The wall seems pretty,
And the room suddenly feels messy.

My mother becomes Hitler,
She's not wrong either.
She says friends are a distraction,
While studying, even the ceiling fan catches my attention.

Every notification, every ding,
Gets you curious,
You randomly start to sing,
And your mother becomes furious.

After school life is easy,
Is the biggest scam!
The thought of university makes me uneasy,
From life now let me scram.

I know this is very sad and relatable,
But this is just a phase,
One day we all will all be fine and stable,
And we'll look back to thank these days.

~*~

24. It's not the end

When everyone's around,
But you feel alone.
When you're amidst all the noise and sound,
Yet it all feels unknown.

When everyone's laughing,
And you're sitting silent.
When you're lagging,
But still have to stay compliant.

When they say you're lazy,
And that you're being ignorant.
But everything seems hazy,
And you no longer feel important.

When you see others achieve,
While you sit and stare.
No one sees you grieve,
About how you feel, not a soul is aware.

You too have goals and dreams,
And work towards them even though it's tough.
You rise as the sun gleams,
Then why does nothing ever feel enough?

When you have lost inspiration,
And they call you a sloth.
But you've got your imagination,
That runs through your mind non-stop.

So being a little slow
Or astray is not the end.
Because this is how we all grow,
It's a new chapter, my friend.

~*~

25. Reminiscence

All the boys and girls now, so mature and poise,
Oh for those days when classrooms were filled with noise!
Food aroma and chalk dust in the air,
Trying to challenge gravity by rocking on your chair.

Munching on food or passing a chit,
And testing the teacher's patience to the very last bit.
Torn pages and soiled garments,
And running to your friends in different classes and departments.

The courage to ask a doubt or visit the staffroom,
To getting lost on your trip back from the washroom.
The canteens were like blessings,
And the fun race back to class once the bell rings.

.Playing cricket with books and mats,
To almost dozing off during maths.
Running to the field to play games,
To knowing each and every classmate and teacher's name.

We began with ABC and 123,
And now learning statistics, geometry, and psychology.
15 years of school life is a journey bittersweet,
Now we wonder, when would we next meet?

Graduation ceremony and a farewell,
Where each student has their own story to tell.
We would never forget anything or anyone,
Hope to see my classmates one day in life's long run!

~*~

26. What went wrong?

Constant glances,
Waiting for just one text.
How many more chances,
Do you expect?

You said you were busy,
And had no time for me.
Then why are you tagged on their story?
Why can't you just set me free?

My family, they all know you,
And talk about you too,
But I had no clue,
That we were soon going to bid adieu.

What went wrong?
Was my everyday question.
Did you make me strong,
Just to fight for your attention?

Was I too clingy?
Or was I ever nosy?
Maybe you thought I was dingy,
Because you were a coward and a phoney.

Well, now I know,
Friendship has limits too.
So I shall breakthrough,
And never cross paths again with you.

~*~

27. Started with a 'Hey'

Nervous and innocent faces,
Just a glance here and there.
All of us from different places,
About the future, we were all unaware.

Started with a 'Hey',
And soon got fond.
Now there's not a single day,
I can live without you around.

All the money spent on phone calls,
All the texts every day.
Laughing through the campus halls,
Because we were late, anyway.

Sharing snacks during class,
And sneaking phones inside.
Cheating sometimes so that we pass,
Each one of us some or the other time lied.

Doodling or playing X and O,
And screaming over a game of hangman.
Fun times as we know,
Were the songs sung in the picnic van.

Oh the poor textbooks,
That came to use the night before an exam.
While teachers gave us glaring looks,
Whenever we were late and said 'Forgive us for the last time ma'am'.

Projects completed together on Zoom,
Was a slap to plagiarism.
Wanting to sneak out of the classroom,
Whenever we were taught about behaviour and mannerism.

Sharing secrets,
And hot gossip spams.
Never forgetting picture credits,
And tagging each other on Instagram.

We may stay together,
We may not too.
Life will get tougher and crazier altogether,
But you will always and forever stay my one and only 'CHINGU'!

~*~

28. Te Amo Mi Amor

Even though it was arranged,
It was like they were meant to be.
On a lovely day, the rings were exchanged,
And soon they started their own little family.

Strangers to lovers,
As all the stories say.
He welcomed her home as she left hers,
And came to stay here with him oh so far away.

One year down the lane,
They found some good news.
Though as usual pregnancy was insane,
But soon life was filled with happy hues.

As the little flower bloomed,
So did their life.
They'd save the little one from every wound,
And together stayed away from every strife.

Though they do bicker,
But more like children.
And sometimes also snicker,
But in the end, give in.

The cuddles every night,
And some sneaky romance,
Kept their relationship cheerful and bright,
That you can see and feel it with just a glance.

They might see the last sunrise together,
While being wrapped in each other's arms.
And levitate from the tensions that bother,
And be blessed and protected in the almighty's arms.

~*~

29. Shattered Mirror

Shaking hands,
And shivering spines.
Pressured by demands,
While the world calmly reclines.

The wrinkled forehead,
With all the worry.
The anxiety ahead,
Which is oh so dreary!

The word 'perfect',
Is always desired.
Will anyone accept,
That I am differently wired?

Laid-back hope,
And shattered mirrors.
Do I blame my horoscope?
Or my fears and terrors?

Wanted to be the lead,
But felt like the second option.
Does anyone pay any heed,
To my words and emotion?

Here I write my woes,
For the world to see and relate.
But only God knows,
When my life would actually escalate.

~*~

30. Grew Apart

People we know the longest,
People who seem to be the best.
Sometimes, they change their path,
And that's how friends grow apart.

From kindergarten to senior high,
A day without them doesn't go by.
But sometimes they stop reciprocating,
And there's a change of emotion and feeling.

From 'you're my soul mate',
To, 'it's best that our ways are separate'.
I had someone to lean on,
But now they're just quietly gone.

Was it my fault or not?
And tons of other questions I've got.
That's why humans need a reason and closure,
So that we can keep our minds and composure.

Best friends to strangers,
I'll no longer be there to protect you from dangers.
You left me without a valid reason,
And I consider that as your biggest treason.

If we cross paths in the future don't say 'hi',
Because you didn't leave me with a better 'goodbye'.
I hope you have a life of good wishes and benefits,
But from now on, don't ever picture me in it.

~*~

31. Don't Fret

Getting out of your comfort zone,
Gossip and drama are all that you've known.
Come so far, yet you feel all alone,
Will you have the chance to survive on your own?

Known faces make anxiety less,
And if we grow apart
Insecurity is a known stress,
They say, "It's just the beginning sweetheart".

A smile on your face 24/7,
And finding topics that interest others.
Cause it's all about the first impression,
And a train of overthinking that bothers.

First day and a fresh start,
Should be happy right?
'Who am I' or 'What's my part?',
Would take up all my might.

You do make friends,
And somehow get along.
But what if people only pretend?
And life is not such a merry song.

Hope is all that keeps you strong,
Along with a positive mindset.
Cause no one can completely define right or wrong,
So breathe, and don't fret.

~*~

32. Kismet Connection

Do you believe in fate?
Or the thought of having a soul mate?
It's never too late,
To find the one, with whom you can relate.

The red string belief,
Gives me hope and relief.
To know there's someone out there,
A gem too rare.

A lover or a friend,
With whom you can share and spend.
A relative or family,
A person with whom you can be lively.

Long talks or just expressions,
That person will understand all your moods and dimensions.
Who understands you the best,
And will always shine amongst the rest.

Your eyes sparkle when they're around,
And you smile just by hearing their voices and sound.
The one who will protect you always,
And stay with you on both your best and worst days.

We often consider our partner as the one,
But your soul mate can be anyone.
With them, you can forever be transparent,
And they shall embrace all your insecurities and embarrassment.

~*~

33. Pitter-Patter

Pitter-patter here and there,
Let's make some hot chocolate.
Enjoying is better when we share,
Why stay gloomy or desolate?

Jumping in muddy puddles,
And clothes filled with dirt.
Or comfy pajamas and cuddles,
While the soil quenches it's thirst.

Snacks and marshmallows,
Make things better.
I forget all my woes,
When I embrace this weather.

The frogs come out,
The plants are all fresh.
There's no doubt,
That we too refresh.

The farmers are all happy,
The peacocks spread their feathers and dance.
Though the surrounding is soggy,
It's the perfect time to romance.

This weather is happy yet calm,
Because the thinkers start their journey.
The raindrops falling on my palm,
Yet tomorrow we're all going to be in a hurry.

~*~

34. Envisage

Do you think the stars feel lonely?
Tired of shining so bright.
Seven billion but why am I the only,
Trying to see their light?

The moon has the star's company,
The sun ignites them both.
In this world full of politics and money,
All I see is jealousy and loathe.

A worthy companion,
Someone who understands without words.
Who wouldn't abandon,
But flock together like birds.

Stargazing, as I look around,
To see no one in sight.
Is this to what, I'm bound?
Is this going to be my plight?

Some questions don't have an answer,
Some people are never found.
A poet is like a freelancer,
Whose feet never touch the ground.

Even though I stargaze alone,
I'd make the most of it.
Why sit and mourn?
When you can enjoy every single bit.

~*~

35. Life Untold

Smile and they think you're happy,
Smile, it'll hide the scar.
Smile and act chirpy,
Till they name you as the brightest star.

Smiling makes you look confident,
And seem attractive.
Even though you don't feel it,
And everything around is refractive.

The three-face theory,
As the Japanese story tells.
Talks about people's misery,
Which prolongs till you hear their final bells.

The world thinks that you're bright,
And hasn't heard your story.
They haven't seen that sight,
Where you're sad and weary.

Life untold,
Is the sight you see in your mirror.
Don't expect it to be tinted gold,
As the hope will only bring you terror.

Go on smiling as they say,
You were born alone and will die alone.
And in the end, it's going to be that way.

~*~

36. Beyond the limit

Expectations tend to be high,
"I don't care", would be a lie.
Nothing seems to go your way,
And none of them is your day.

Should I change my priority?
And show you my maturity.
If I care, am I childish?
But thinking about you makes my mind go wildish.

If I am concerned, I seem nosy,
Where are those days that were oh so rosy?
Group view shows the power of the majority,
If I don't agree, do I seem like a liability?

Skipping my way through life isn't really possible,
Is my jealousy no longer justifiable?
Your person ain't yours anymore,
And all you see is another closed door.

Forever is a myth, nothing lasts long,
So keeping any hope, on my part, is wrong.
I will think about and love you forever,
But by circumstances I know, be with you never.

~*~

37. 100 Reasons

I gave myself 100 reasons to love you,
But you didn't want any.
Wished all my desires and fantasies to come true,
But you didn't care a penny.

Lovesick and lost,
That's what I became.
All this at what cost?
When you didn't even remember my name.

Spammed your messages,
Is that why?
You'd see them after ages,
Without a single reply.

If I disappear,
Would you care?
As whenever I was near,
You were never aware.

They call it one-sided,
But I knew my feelings were highly involved.
In you, I confided,
And around you, my life revolved.

Been many people's cupid,
Is there a match made for me?
Look how your love made me, oh so stupid!
Will I ever have you in my love story?

~*~

38. Go?

They say beauty lies in the eyes of the beholder,
Then why do we feel insecure, as and when we grow older?
We all have different scars and marks,
Then why does one judge and pass comments and remarks?

They say to study to have a better future,
But what if I am a defect in manufacture?
Go by the rules, that's not what I like,
If each home run matters, then so does every strike.

A calming atmosphere and a peaceful walk,
Sometimes silence or a person to talk?
If I am happy, are you?
Sometimes we try to fit in by adjusting to what's new.

Does sugar and spice make a perfect balance?
Does a degree plus a job only prove my intelligence?
Following footsteps while creating your own path,
Or following the society to stay away from the wrath.

From being toddlers to adults there is a certain pain,
That we face no matter if there's sun or rain.
Is it I, or me who lacks?
Is it that impossible to lay your own tracks?

Coming and going is like part and parcel,
Is there a button to turn back and fix everything crucial?
Opportunities come either very fast or comparatively slow,
It depends on us whether we choose to pause, rewind or go!

~*~

39. Dear Diary

How was your day?
Oh, what should I say?
Hectic schedules,
And too many rules.

So many people around,
But my mind ain't sound.
Walk away,
Or should I stay?

Flew with the wind,
While my phone dinged.
I went to type 'Hi',
But I guess it was time to say goodbye.

Looked at a sparkling sight,
While my heart and mind had a fight.
Thought about how my life became weary,
But in the end, I still had my 'Dear Diary'.

~*~

The Continuation

This journey is a never-ending one, as I haven't given up on writing. Though all writers have mind blocks, steadily regaining our passion allows this journey to continue. Thanks for following my journey this far >.<

40. Body Positivity?

World let's have a chat,
Hair is just hair.
Getting judged for that,
It's just not fair.

Staring at someone,
Or just taking a look.
Society you spared none,
And no flaw can be overlooked.

Smooth legs and hands,
Is that all you expect?
Even after trying uncountable brands,
What if I have side effects?

They say love your body,
Or promote body positivity.
It's ok for skin to look bumpy,
Biased thoughts are what I pity.

The time that's lost,
And the pain that's felt.
Applying creams that cost,
So that the wounds are dealt.

Can painful thoughts turn back?
Can positivity be spread?
It is not beauty that we lack,
So let us together break this thread.

~*~

41. A love letter to Cinema

Started in 1895,
From black and white to colour.
Your popularity spread far and wide,
And in 2004 was the birth of your lover.

I haven't seen your previous side,
But loved you passionately enough.
Your journey so far has been a long ride,
Across the different screens that you engulf.

Be it tragedy or romance,
You have given the people variety.
The reason why you have so many fans,
Is because though out of the box, you portray propriety.

You gave life to imagination,
To the cast, crew, and the entire team.
That they work hard for every creation,
To make the audience applaud and scream.

Love can't be measured in words,
But can be seen through actions.
While you connect different worlds,
We give you our best reactions.

Though it ain't the best,
But I wrote you this letter.
That cinema surpassed the rest,
And it just keeps getting better.

~*~

42. Sunshine and rainbows?

Things happen for a reason,
You can't change the past.
You can't alter any season,
Nor completely predict a forecast.

Fire can burn a forest,
Or light a person's home.
Some things we try to do the best.
Become the reason of a deadly syndrome.

It's impossible to predict our future,
If we're not vigilant in our present.
Our life is ours to nurture,
And our choice if it's dull or fluorescent.

Problems come and go,
There's always a new day.
To the negativity, we can say no,
And face the hardships to go away.

Sunshine and rainbows are not constant,
Nothing stays the same.
But if we stay persistent,
We can excel in life's game.

I may not give a solution,
But I try to advise.
Because life ain't about a conclusion,
We can only try to ski through the ice.

~*~

43. Letters hidden between books

Long-buried feelings,
Held captive in pages worn out.
The paintings on the ceilings,
Were marvellous stories no doubt.

Letters hidden between books,
Some the owner never found.
Passing each other fluttering looks,
While the feet of joy didn't touch the ground.

A simple smile, you could tell,
Got them all anticipated.
But none of us can now tell,
How long they must have waited.

The adventurous thought,
Came with feelings that could scare.
But they cherished whatever they got,
Because it was an affair.

She would be called characterless,
And in the village, he'd be forlorn.
But they couldn't care less,
As love was everything they've known.

They might have drifted,
Or eloped together.
Now nobody knows they existed,
Or about their love that didn't wither.

~*~

44. Silent wet pillows

From loud rattling cries,
To silent wet pillows.
Filled with grey skies,
And wilting dead willows.

A breath of relief,
Dominated by a sigh.
The forehead shows grief,
While the heart wants to die.

From fingers crossed,
To hands now scratched.
The purpose now lost,
And the confidence snatched.

From colour to grey,
No sparkles only black.
Nothing left to say,
Never want to be back.

Being invisible is an art,
That people make of each other.
It takes them seconds to depart,
And scare and scar forever.

The smoke inhaled,
The intoxicant now swallowed.
To the cross, I'd rather be nailed,
Away from all the physical load.

~*~

45. Gender Roles

You treated me like a little lady,
And wrapped me in a pretty frock.
But you didn't tell me that the world is shady,
And to protect myself, I should live under a rock.

The gender roles confused me,
While I sat straight with my knees joined.
While the superiors were left free,
We are equally capable but what's the point?

Tight dresses to fit each curve,
And look like a modest female.
What purpose do I serve?
If I am dominated enough to derail.

A light colour makes one look pretty,
While dark ones are too bold.
These norms were and are too petty,
Every person is worthier than gold.

The world wants a hole,
Who hushes their voice in and out.
No one respects the whole,
And you are overreacting if you shout.

One question never answered, then and now,
Was, why do all these roles matter?
We'd keep asking them when and how?
But only silence is heard from the latter.

~*~

46. Delulu

Honeybun or your darling,
I waited for you so long.
Now I want you to give me that ring,
For which I dearly long.

The alarm rings,
Another dream was left unended.
No birds for me that sing,
Nor a charming prince so splendid.

No balls for me to attend,
And dress up all pretty.
No gowns to mend,
Oh, what a pity!

No butterflies in my gut,
Nor a lovely stranger.
All this I wish, but,
Destiny is not for me but her.

You are fictional,
But I thought of you as mine,
I'd love you unconditional,
Till the novel's very last line.

~*~

47. Boundaries

Their lips met mine,
It felt so divine.
An action so simple,
Ran down shivers like a ripple.

The soothing aromatic candle,
Didn't help sensations I couldn't handle.
The tension in between,
And the explicit view I had seen.

But then I went blank,
And soon my heart sank.
You gave me no butterflies,
And in your mouth died down my cries.

The slight push I gave,
Boosted the lust that you crave.
You didn't understand when I said no,
Took it as a heads-up and continued to go.

No, I didn't lose the affection,
But I did have an objection.
Together we belong,
But some things are just so wrong.

Love too has a boundary,
And feelings are scary.
Just for love, I won't give in,
Cause no consent, is a sin.

~*~

48. A visitor for the heart

What is this feeling?
Am I in love?
But my heart's still healing,
From the dark clouds above.

That echoing laughter,
And those twinkling eyes.
As my heart keeps beating faster,
While my alarm loudly cries.

I dreamt about you again today,
Been this way too long.
Oh, that one glimpse that day,
Replays in my mind all along.

Met as a matter of chance,
You said we'd meet again.
So every day I glance,
At your socials in vain.

You are not my fantasy,
But not less than a dream.
As you put me in a state of ecstasy,
And in joy I squeal and scream.

This time I won't be late,
And grab the opportunity.
As I look forward to our next date,
And anticipate in glee.

~*~

49. Smiling away with you

No matter how much water you give a plucked rose,
It will wilt.
Similarly, why don't we care about those
Relationships that we have built?

Somehow we always neglect,
The ones who care the most.
And then sit and repent,
When the person becomes a ghost.

How funny are our emotions,
That act up anytime.
While we carry out certain actions,
That are far from not fine.

Crazy how we all know this,
But cannot change a thing.
If we all continue like this,
There wouldn't even be any last string.

Do you change yourself?
Or the actions you do?
Cause soon we will all be pictures on the shelf,
And become just names too.

So maybe if I say sorry,
And mean it through my actions too,
We would have lesser things to worry,
While I am smiling away with you.

~*~

50. From the Shadows

Knives, pencils and even her teeth,
She left nothing at all.
Wounds above and beneath,
While the silent tears would fall.

Was that right?
Isn't even the question anymore.
Because her hands were always clutched tight,
While her discipline people would adore.

A good person, was what mother said,
Would the world befriend.
But the silent screams while she lay in bed,
Was this going to be her end?

'Certainly not', said a little voice,
Ringing in her head.
She had to make the choice,
If she wanted life to move ahead.

So she tied her hair,
And walked to her friends.
While her demons would stare,
As she was trying to make amends.

Asking for help wasn't the problem,
But fear of change, was scary.
As she also risked the outcome,
But it's not the end of her story.

She found hope, she found a light,
A hand that held her close.
There are several people who might,
Care about you from the shadows.

~*~

51. Smile today

Why do we wait for a happily ever after?
Or any ending at all?
Let us fill our lives with laughter,
Just live for ourselves and not to enthral.

Human emotions are weird,
We cry when we're happy, sad, and even angry.
The future is feared,
And the present is weary.

People say 'Go get a life',
And that 'You're so nosy'.
People or things that made you feel alive,
Now seem dull and lousy.

Happiness is what we all seek,
While sadness we shun.
Life may have turned bleak,
And we are no longer comforted by anyone.

You're in the ditch waiting for a hand,
Who'd bring you out and be your saviour,
But what if you're stuck in quick sand?
From where you won't return forever.

It's good to desire for the best,
And hope for it too.
Let's just forget about the rest,
And smile today, just for yourself, and only for you!

~*~

Epilogue

This feels incomplete right?

Hmm, looks like we have reached the end of this book, but our journey doesn't end here.

This poet will be back.

See you in the next book!

Love XOXO,

Nurain

About The Author

Nurain FK

Nurain by day, a psychology student embracing her roles as a friend and daughter; by night, a poet weaving words under the moon. She dives into books, spills emotions onto pages, and swirls colors on canvases, finding comfort in art and music. For her, human potential is a boundless sea of creativity, ready to be explored through writing, art, and more.

www.ingramcontent.com/pod-product-compliance
Lightning Source LLC
LaVergne TN
LVHW041115150826
845673LV00007B/2056

9798892774185